MOONLIGHT AND MONSTERS

For my grandmother, Maria Guadalupe Arroyo, and for my great-grandmother, Lucy Herrera Arroyo.

Praise for *Moonlight and Monsters*

In *Moonlight and Monsters*, Lauren Scharhag dives into the spectral pools of everyday and brings us "rainbows embedded in grackle darkness." And when she dives, she brings the whole flaming, gutted church to its knees to feed "...creatures that some call pests and some call mischief, some call God." She guides us into the echoing velvet hallways of her Hispanic heritage and we are mauled by the nagual, we drown with La Llorona, we fall under the spell of ambergris-scented brujas. She leads us expertly with her prayers through her sorrows through transmutation into a kind of flashing hope in the ashes, and we cannot save ourselves from being burned clean from the cinders. We willingly follow because "In order to emerge, one must be swallowed whole." Scharhag has birthed a breathing singing thing in this collection, and we feel her labor and tearing of skin, as she explains, "the agony of creation is inescapable." And what she has brought to life is as miraculous as it is rare.

-Scott Ferry, author of *The Long Blade of Days Ahead*

These poems exist somewhere between the world of fairy-tale and a woman at a kitchen counter slicing salami with an old Windows XP disc. Scharhag writes with unsettling intimacy, teetering between the unconscious and that place where we wear jungle air like wet silk. She invites us into the extended night of the tomb where men are just beasts in textiles, where words flicker, illuminate and delight. It's hard chasing shadows in these well-lit times, but if we allow ourselves, however briefly, to see the world through Scharhag's eyes, the portal might just open to let in all that tremulous beauty and wonder.

-Lillian Necakov, author of *il virus*

Lauren Scharhag writes about people and the facets of psyche that knit them together. A true collector, she hordes the bits and pieces and puts them on display in her poetry. As she herself says in "Hair Work," this collection spins many parts into a cohesive unit "like spider silk, connecting the living and the living, and the living with the dead." Digging deep, Scharhag unearths the vital that runs through us, finding us where we are, and as we are. Here lies a poet's heart, bruised but still beating.

-Angela Yuriko Smith, Bram Stoker Award-winning author and publisher of *Space & Time* Magazine

Table of Contents

MOONLIGHT

Necromancy

after Anatomical Venuses, 18th century

It was the Enlightenment. For science, they said. For art.
For God. For the body is the reflection of the world, is
a reflection of God. (As above, so below.) They sought
the pinnacle of knowledge. But cadavers were hard to come by.
So the artists came, the ceroplasticians, pouring beeswax
and chemicals into molds, conjuring Pygmalion's nameless love.
We emerged, a spill of curls, a throat of pearls, hips and breasts,
inlaid glass eyes lined with real lashes, recumbent like Odalisques,
heads thrown back, arms behind our heads, painted faces both
ecstatic and serene, Holy Virgins receiving our Annunciations,
even the pregnant models. Invariably white as ivory, invariably
slender,
invariably comely. For the anatomy lessons, they said, but only
female figures were rendered in such meticulous detail. The males
were skinless, featureless, prosaic. But we have our own magic.
We know about effigies. We know about simulacrums.
We know about golems and fertility statues. You peeled
back the layers, tunneled into us, trying to understand.
Look how these organs unfurl. Look at this fetus, so realistic.
You called us Venuses. You named us for a goddess, the one
that shares her name with *veneration*. But we had no say.
And we held the wrong kind of sway. You knelt at our sides,
knowing it was a false love, a false idolatry. But the hatred
was real, the contempt was real, as it was in the beginning,
now and ever shall be. You called us slashed beauties.
Thoraxes and abdomens sprung like the lid of a pocket watch.
Or like the lid torn off of Pandora's box. Perhaps you denied
the sexual nature, perhaps you reveled in it, perhaps both. We are
creatures of infinite contradiction, of infinite appetite. Did you
know
the word agalmatophilia? Did you know it was necromancy? We
were
the forbidden. Faux dead, for real damned. We were the uncanny
valley
and you went blithely down, exposing that which was once hidden.
The violence and the violation. Such transgressions exact their price,

O, Liebestod. O, Rohypnol. See us. Know our names: Elizabeth Smart.
Jon Benet Ramsey, Laura Palmer, Marilyn Monroe, Mary Ann
Nichols,
Ophelia, Snow White, Annabel Lee, Zellandine/Aurora/Briar Rose.
The dead beauty is the eternal beauty, or so you say. What women
ought to be, and what we ought not to be. The bed is a coffin. To die
is to become an object. No matter what, beautiful women especially
are thought to be complicit in their own demise. We should be
thanking
the men who bestowed the gift of their attention, froze us in time,
spared us
crow's feet and saggy tits. Pardon our lack of gratitude. We are only
made of wax and a single rib.

Alligator Tooth
a cadralor

1. Redbud
My grandfather wants a tree for his yard. We ride in the old
Cheyenne.
I must've been small, my brother yet unborn, and I don't know these
highways.
I never knew my grandfather to leave the city except twice, to return
to Mexico.
He'd bring back Michoacán quince and coconut candies, and leche
quemada that I,
ruined on Hershey's, could never hope to appreciate.
He digs up a redbud and hauls it back in the rusty truck bed.
He plants it next to the garden gate.
I grow with it and in it, my shadow swallowed up by its shadow,
my bed strewn violet-pink. Sometimes, you uproot what you desire.

2. Festival
Autumn, and festivals descend
with their ciders and kitsch and octopus rides.
In the throes of girlhood, I covet abalone jewelry,
entranced by its nacreous hues,
as I am entranced by the rainbows embedded in grackle darkness.
A boy buys me an alligator charm.
The Aztecs said Crocodile was the Earth floating in the primordial
waters,
a being of infinite hunger, a mouth at every joint.
I open and close.

3. Monster
Lost summer afternoons
spent shut up with paperbacks.
Now I am spellbound by vampires
the way some girls love boy bands or ballet or horses.
We all share a desire to escape the mundane.
Girlhood feels like dying all the time.
I want a different kind of dying,
a different kind of blood.

I want to be alabaster.

4. New Orleans
I flee to Mardi Gras— south, but not south enough.
Beads brighten wrought-iron fences and February trees. I am alone in
the drunk crowd.
Haunted tours meet up at Jackson Square, in front of voodoo shops.
That's where he finds me, gripping a fetish bag.
His beauty is like the glint off quartz, like the turn of a fortune
teller's card,
fleeting, beguiling.
There are drapes on the four-poster bed. My desire is opalescent in
the darkness.
I will return to the long fast.
The ashes will come.

5. Contrition
No one told me desire was a path.
No one said that everywhere I went, I'd be looking for home,
and everyone I met, I'd be searching their faces
for something familiar,
a taste of scalded milk, the scent of burning palm leaves.
My rosary strung with hollow teeth.
I detest all my sins.
I weep redbud tears as I beg,
Blood of my blood, please, let me return to you.

Confiscated
after El Sueño Americano | The American Dream: Photographs by Tom
Kiefer

No one hides from the man with the broom.
Whatever we consume, the evidence eventually
finds its way into his bins,
detritus of our cruel and greedy hearts.

Nonessential, the officers say, or
Potential lethal weapons.

Confiscate.

It begins with the general:
items that can be bought anywhere,
from any gas station
or Motel 6 vending machine
or Dollar Store.
They could belong to anyone.

Toothbrushes. Tubes of toothpaste.
Rolls of toilet paper. Bars of soap.
Condoms. Foot powder.
An assortment of combs and brushes,
hair no doubt still clinging
to bristles and teeth. *Nonessential.*

He is unable to bring himself
to throw it all away,
items someone saw fit to carry
as far as 2,500 hundred miles,
little bits of comfort
on a hard and dangerous trek.

Next are survival items: still impersonal.
Flatware. Bottled water and canteens.
Blankets. Canned food.
(Many varieties of Tuny's for easy protein.)

Snickers bars. *Nonessential.*

For a time, he collects the nonperishables
to donate to a local food bank,
until the facility comes under new management
and they make him stop.
That is not the service they pay him to perform.
Nonessential.

Now we're verging on the personal:
blister packs of medication.
Birth control pills. Prozac. Insulin.
You wonder what's become of their wellness.
Nonessential.

Belts and shoelaces. *Potential weapons.*

Cell phones and chargers,
CDs on a dream-pink backdrop:
Boogie Nights. Trapt.
Somebody's burn mix labelled, *Brown Pride.*
Wallets. Striped polos. *Nonessential.*

Work gloves. Pocketknives and multi-tools,
probably necessary for crossing
mountains and deserts, probably
in anticipation of the hard labor
they've come to seek.
Potential weapons.

Rosaries coiled on a gray field,
absent fingers and mouths to pray them;
Blue Bibles on a yellow bandana,
Virgin of Guadalupe statues.
The soul. *Nonessential.*

At last, we've arrived at the intimate:
unfolding the gold-locket heart of it,
photos, a handwritten love letter,

tuyo siempre.
But what has become of the hand,
and what of John 13 and 15?
1 Corinthians 13? Luke 6:31?
Nonessential.

Rubber duckies.
A single toddler's shoe.

When do things stop being things
and graduate
to artifact?

10,000 objects salvaged,
such a small collection,
even fewer made poignant
beneath his lens.

Imagine 10,000 pairs of hands.
Imagine 5,000,000 steps.

Confiscated. Thrown out.

Now imagine
salvage and salvation.

Essential. Shields.

Asylum Prayer

Say, God is meaningless,
unless They know our pain.
Say, this is the selling point of Christ,
a god who is also a bleeder,
a laborer, a partaker of bread,
a refugee.

Say, this is my exhaustion:
searching for the godlike
in the faces of corruption,
in the places of razor wire.
Say, mothers, your milk
dries as tears. Say, children,
we are all out of lullabies.
Say, Samaritans, keep your gifts.

Say, this desert air
is the breath of God.
If you want baptism,
here is the indifferent river,
the toilet basin.

Say, this want
is an emanation of God.
Say, the Dollar Almighty
has its chosen people.
Even the haven of light
will be denied,
the all-knowing motion sensors,
the bulbs that rob the weary
of sleep, dreams, time,
those most fundamental of healers.

Say that despair is the soul-killer,
the looking away. Say, we must
be bigger than God. Say,
we must do what God cannot.

We must be here, in the flesh.
Our persistence must be so great,
even They will be humbled.

Portrait of an Amateur Roadkill Artist

After the divorce, there were the standard
every-other-weekend visitations.
My father would come to pick me up
and we'd spend the day driving around
back country roads in his old Datsun
with no air conditioning, windows down.
He had a new-to-him camera, and was searching,
searching, as he'd searched his whole life.
He'd come from a family of artists,
and was cursed with the temperament.
He tried law school and business school,
tried the Air Force, tried to be a writer,
tried to work for his father's friends,
tried to own his own business, tried
to be a rancher, a farmer, a mortician,
a house husband. Nothing stuck.
On those sunny blue days, we stopped
for broken-down old barns or brick silos
grown over with ivy or just empty pastures
that caught his eye. I was seven, and unspeakably
bored, leaning against split-rail fences.
What's so special, I asked, *about some old barn?*
I'm not sure he ever answered. We went
to the movies. He'd buy us a ticket,
but we never watched just one. *Double feature,*
he always said. He cried all through *Philadelphia.*
I remember his old three-story walk-up,
the warped floorboards that felt like
they could give out from under my feet
at any time. Then our day trips were spent
searching for roadkill. I looked away
anytime he found a patch of blood
and ruined fur baked into the asphalt.
Why? I asked as his camera whirred
and clicked. *Look at their expressions,*
he laughed. *Just look at them.*
He struck out west. There was another wife,

another child, another girlfriend, California,
where he lived in his car for two years.
I saw him less and less. Five other states,
New York, last I heard. Did you ever
find what it was you were looking for?
Look at my expression. I get it now.
The dead don't look back.

The Twelfth of Never

Your third marriage was surely
still in its honeymoon phase
when Johnny Mathis crooned
about unending love.
I never knew whether to
admire your commitment
to finding The One
or to shudder
at the desperation
casting a pall
on this time's charms.

By the time I came along,
full of the questions children ask,
Will I be rich?
Will I be famous?
Will I fall in love?

You had an answer ready:
Sure, kid. On the twelfth of never.

When the last husband up and left,
people asked if you thought
he'd come back.
You told them the same.
You said it so much I thought
you'd invented the phrase.
Yet, you kept his picture
under your pillow,
and quit leaving the house
in case he returned.

Twenty-two years of
hovering by the phone,
watching the road for his car,
stopping all the clocks
at the hour of his departure.

And then,
three months after you died,
the letter came.

He, too, had racked up
another divorce or two.
He was just out of prison.
If you would just take him back,
he swore, this time,
it would all be different.
This time, it would be forever.

It was the impossibility
you'd always dismissed:
the bloomless bluebell,
the scentless clover,
the mute scribe.

The twelfth of never
was finally here,
but there was no one
to tell him that
you weren't.

Past Life as a Man

I feel certain that in all my past lives,
I was a man. Not a famous man.
I was never Napoleon or Hitler
or Charlie Manson or Malcolm X
or Picasso or Tolstoy
or Errol Flynn.
I was probably never a looker,
nor a conqueror,
paragon of nothing much.
I'm sure I beat my wife,
raped when I could.
I molded sons in my image
and went off to war.
I'm sure I worked till I dropped
and accepted my lot.
I'm sure I must have brawled
and thrown stones,
plowed fields, raised barns,
attended lectures,
contemplated the stars.
Am I the bitch in karma?
There must be a reason
why this all feels so familiar.
I'm sure I must have placed
and displaced, drag-raced,
disgraced, knocked back,
knocked up, knocked out,
knelt, rose, hunted, trapped,
baited, hooked, fished, stalked,
felt the thrash of life
in my chapped fist.
I think I must have done it
to someone at some point,
so I damn well know
what it looks like
when it gets
done to me.

Knowing You

You don't know
how to dress your new body,
gravitating towards broomstick skirts,
prim florals, pleats and pintucks.
I thought it was part of your charm,
actually, the awkwardness
of a second adolescence,
all elbows and knees and untamed hair.
But how could you know?
You haven't achieved it yet, your body,
swimming towards it, upstream,
a selkie determined
to discard your heavy pelt,
a milkweed pod splitting
because it must
to release its seeds.

I worship at the altar
of your becoming.

How long have you known? I ask.

Since always, you answer.
Maybe even
before I was born.
My spirit was a woman
even before
she was a baby.

I can't imagine
knowing myself
in such a way,
all the way down
to the root.

I undress you and you
undress me.

I see the hormones are working their magic,
bringing out what was there all along:

the softening of jaw and muscle tone,
rounding of torso, cock and balls
shrinking and shriveling in on themselves.
I cup those wizened apricots,
stroke what remains of the peach fuzz
dotting your cheeks,
kiss your ripening mouth.

I had a hysterectomy at 26.
I, too, require pills to maintain
my femininity.

We hold each other, two women;
you even manage
to get it hard for me, for a moment,
and I wonder if it will ever be
in anyone else again,
because the day is coming soon
when you take yourself
into yourself
forever
and you will be whole.

But for now,
let us scatter the bed
with the shards of us.

So much is made
of eternity
the idea of love
as a fixed star,
but we know better.

Let us

become

together

a celebration

of impermanence.

The Unseeing

We see only the bills that need to be paid.
We are consumed with shopping lists and topping off fuel tanks.
At best, we shut off the lights
or we turn off the tap when we brush our teeth.
We are concerned with the lakes where we summer,
with the diminishing songbirds that once
graced our backyard feeders,
with the sea turtles we saw once at an aquarium,
with the deer, suddenly homeless,
crashing through our bay windows
in a violent reversal of life,
afterbirth of blood and glass.
It's hard to imagine the landfills that are kept
well away from our neighborhoods,
the slow boats to China laden with waste
now being marked return to sender.
Most of us have seen more ivory
in our lifetime than elephants,
so how do we conceptualize a glacier,
the groan of a cracking ice shelf?
Most of us will never stand on the thing
that could drown the world,
or even know that the pitcher has been tipped.
The frog can't see the slow boil nor
the grasshopper summer's end.
To everyone, their way of life is forever.
Would we understand better if you told us
Sunday has been cancelled,
that there will be no more Easter egg hunts?
Would we understand what it means to say
this is the death cabinet and we just keep
adding species to it? Somewhere, the last
giraffe does not know it is the last giraffe.
Somewhere, the last unseeing man will come
to his epiphany.

Futility and Other Sins

I have tasted defeat so many times
I can tell you what wine to pair with it.
I have felt futility carve into me
its Sisyphean groove.
I have glimpsed bitterness myopically,
a pair of broken reading glasses
at the end of the world.
Rejection is the dominatrix that stings me
and keeps me coming back for more.
I am not the friend to the downtrodden
I had aspired to be in youth.
I have never been the rescuer
of a single marooned sea star, even
when the opportunity presented itself,
but stood instead on the desolate shore,
as if in a doorway,
awaiting grace or ubuntu to show up
and drag me from my hermitage.
I've wrung every drop from solitude
as I'd wring the juice from a prickly pear,
stranded, parched, along the Devil's Highway.
I cling to apathy the way a passenger
clings to the drop-down oxygen mask
as the jet spirals to the ground,
believing, with a sort of holy urgency,
that I must help me before I help anyone else,
that I cannot pour from an empty cup.
I realize I, too, am a gasping starfish,
a distressed passenger at the mercy of gravity.

The Long Night

It felt like it was always winter
while we waited;
a long, cold intermission.
It always felt like we had to sit
and let the car warm up.
It felt like I always had to drive slow,
mindful of the black ice,
my back tires spinning on hills.

At the hospital, again,
and again, I had to wait
while they got you checked in,
the TV and the lights always set
to the exact same volume: *blare.*
The seating seemed chosen specifically
for its lack of comfort.

The nurses would be positively ghoulish:
It's car accident season, they'd say.
You might get lucky.

Lucky.
When your luck comes only
at someone else's disaster,
can you still call it luck?

There was a waiting room in the renal ward
that was usually empty.
That's where I liked to sit.
I'd look out the window at the snow.
I'd think of the solstice.
I'd think of Yuletide, season of death and life.
I'd think of the hunt.
I'd think of the right confluence of events
that would put an end to our waiting,
one way or the other.

They'd tell me
you were going to be here a while.
That I should go home. Get some sleep.

I wanted to tell them, *I haven't slept
in four years.*

Maybe that's why it also felt
like it was always night.

The Real Meaning of Inferno

Four winters on the transplant list,
and you are always cold. We bundle you
in long johns and sweatshirts, blankets
and stocking caps, and park you next to
a space heater, and still, you shiver, while
I sweat. I sweat the medical bills and the
regular bills and whether you have a fever
again and if you are eating enough and how
are we ever going to pay for more medicine and
the second job I'm going to have to get. I burn
crimson like my grandmother's red Depression
glass oil lamp. I burn blue-white like the
rings on a gas stove. I burn like the gold
and orange flames in the cast-iron furnace where
we used to heat our clothes on winter mornings,
and still get dressed under the quilt. *Inferno*
is a word that's synonymous with hellfire,
but originally, it had nothing to do with heat. It
meant *the lower regions.* I think of this as I go
down into the basement of our sixty-year-old house,
past the cracked walls where slugs and spiders
and snakes slither in, past the exposed foundation
stones and the water stains where it's flooded
each spring, past the shelf where we store
your dialysis supplies, to examine our own
beast of a unit. I've always thought it looked like
Doc Ock if Doc Ock had sprouted a few more arms,
if he'd grown feeble and rickety and might,
at any moment, give up the ghost. If it goes out on us,
no second or even a third job will be enough to help me
replace it. I come back upstairs and make us cups of cocoa.
You tell me how you dream of the sea, of sun-warmed
sand, of tropical paradises. I do not tell you that I dream,
too: nightmares of a furnace-less house in January
and frozen pipes bursting in the walls. Hell isn't hot,
but it's real, and it's here. I crack open a window
far from you and try to breathe. I'm hotter than

particles smashing around the Large Hadron Collider.
I'm hotter than the torch Prometheus saw fit to pilfer.
I'm hotter than molting phoenix feathers. I'm hotter
than a morningstar supernova. If the furnace goes out,
split me like heartwood. I will be your hearth
and your kindling. Cook a meal over my radiance.
Bask in me. I will see you through to summer.

St. Teresa's Day
a cadralor

1. Prostrate
I am seven when the first migraine seizes me in its jaws.
I've spent the night on my grandmother's floor, Sirius prowling the July sky.
Glaring afternoons pass like the whine of a mosquito, the nights craving
the weak gust of a box fan, kicking off sodden sheets, wanting to climb
out of my own skin. Sharing a bed is an impossibility.
I try to raise my head and this, also, proves impossible.
From the kitchen comes the drone of bacon, my grandmother's voice
telling me to come eat. The world has become unbearable.
If I could form a thought, it would be only to find some way of escaping it.
The pain is almost mystic, a seraph's spear piercing my skull, a holy trepanation.

2. Goya's Dog
At a discoteca in Madrid, a boy wants to kiss me, and I dance away.
I live for the open air mercados, lunching on manchego and baguette slices.
In Puerto de Lapices, I eat green olives from the grove outside.
I make my pilgrimage to the Prado,
soaking in the cool dark, the cathedral silence.
Its masters, Velazquez and Bosch and El Greco, await my adoration.
Goya haunts me, especially the dog, alone,
looking up at something only he can see.
I'm afraid to be the dog, alone with my visions,
at the mercy of my senses, at the mercy of everything.

3. Cherries
The apartment behind the club. Our balcony faced the alley.
Throb of bass every night, drunks fighting and vomiting over the fence,
tinkle and crash of bottles. Nonetheless, we strung up a hammock.

There was a fruit and flower stand on the corner.
We bought a basket of cherries, and two bougainvillea that bloomed
impossible shades of heliotrope and Fanta orange all summer.
We swung beneath them, petals falling on our faces.
I spat cherry pits over the railing, hoping that one of them
would take root, a childish wish for a tiny oasis,
lush leaves and ruby fruit.

4. The Blue Ridge
The year my father and I road tripped along the Blue Ridge,
I could barely take in the spectacle of it: lowland fields of sunflowers,
bursts of cattle birds, white as salvation, and runnels of water
cascading down out of the granite steeps. At a roadside stand,
a solitary woman sells peaches. She offers us three bushels
in exchange for my father's collie. No deal. We buy the peaches outright,
our hands stained with their juice all the way to Asheville, stickying the seats.
It starts to rain. Homeless men huddle around a metal trashcan fire.
I skip stones across the Shenandoah. The mist is a cool hand on my brow.
I can breathe here. In these woad-colored mountains, I can breathe.

5. Deliverance
The night the call came from the transplant center, sleep was out of the question.
So I cleaned the kitchen, folded laundry, my mind blank with terror.
Someone had died. Someone had died so that we might live.
A thief in the night stolen in. I look up, my head a fruit that's gone soft,
pulp ready to yield up the hardness at its center. You were not with me,
in the mountains, in the marble halls, but you were. You were not with me
on the shag rug of my agony, but you were. All that pain, all the panic and paralysis,

all the prayers, all the bargains I'd made with the universe. (If I deny myself this,
my reward will be that much the sweeter.) This is what I'd been waiting for.
Tomorrow, in the operating room, I won't be with you, but I will be. I will be with you.

Orenda

Inherent power:
the old ones knew
there was something
more democratic
about giving every
natural thing
a stake in it.
It pleases me
to think that stone
and mist,
flame and dew
are no less deserving
for lacking breath.

Veladoras

At the Dollar General,
they sell saint candles
in the Hispanic aisle
alongside bags of beans and rice:
La Virgen de Guadalupe next to boxes
of Abuelita chocolate,
Sacred Heart Jesus by the Maseca
St. Anthony among the canned nopales.
St. Christopher got demoted,
but is accounted for nonetheless
alongside hominy and St. Jude.
I load my cart with them, a dollar apiece,
comfort and comfort food,
some traditions unkillable even though
I stay far away from the confessional
and the last true believer in our family
died ten years ago.

Baby's Breath
a cadralor

1. Lake Jacomo
You are horrified to learn I've never been camping. I'm a city kid.
The idea of going beyond where the streetlights end creeps me out.
You promise to start me off gently. We buy gear and drive out to the
lake, with its marina and bathroom facilities. We pitch our little red
tent for two and build the fire. And by "we" I mean "you." The
honeysuckle bushes are in bloom, white and gold. In the chill of dusk,
you cover me with an old fleece blanket. I'm fine until I try to sleep
on the ground, which is hard and cold and this is why we bury dead
things in it. Someone from the next site over is snoring like a weed
whacker. I wake you and say, like a child, "I want to go home." And
of course, you take me home, uncomplaining, even though it means
rising in the predawn hours to pack everything up. For days after,
your jacket smells of campfire smoke. That's outdoors enough for me.

2. Lammas
When the scales are about to tip in night's favor, I am a priestess of
corn tortillas and Dos Equis. At sunset, I go out to a field, raked
smooth and brown as a carob pod. This is not my natural habitat; I
am a creature of the hearth. But if my hands can knead masa, they
can learn to sift this loam. Once, my grandmother carried both my
mother and me. I carry nothing but my meager offerings. I set up
my altar and light the candles. I tell the field, I have tried not to sow
regret. When spring comes again, these acres will grow deep with
prairie grass, with golden compass plant and purple coneflower. I
kneel, my mouth full of seeds, and am rewarded with visions of a
green man. He assures me that the agony of creation is inescapable.
Plant fish with the corn. Hunt for morels when the forest fires have
burned out. We are both blade of grass and blade of scythe, debtor
and debt. Don't forget to pay what you owe.

3. Crystal River
Facedown in the jade-colored cove, winter sun on our backs, trying
to imitate the way manatees and their calves float along the bottom,
trying to lure them from their avid grazing, fingers aching to touch
their barnacled sides. The water is so cold, when you climb in, it stuns

you. The unfamiliar cling of the wetsuit reinforces the sensation, like a strange rebirth. You want to splash and flail, but you don't want to frighten the creatures away. You don't want to stir up silt and obscure them from view. Man is not the leading cause of manatee death, but pneumonia. Which is not to say we don't hurt them, because of course we do. In fact, we identify them by their scar patterns. I can't take the mask and the snorkeling gear. I can't take this dead man's float. I panic, a violent pulmonary action, like the storms that suck the river out to sea, leaving the channels dry. Clambering back into the boat, I strip it all off and lie gasping on the boards.

4. Black Friday
We keep thinking that malls are over, but today, this one is awash with shoppers
in their parkas and scarves. Somewhere, a Wurlitzer is playing, clashing
with the piped-in Christmas music. Still, the lights dazzle. Toy stores seem to burn
the brightest. From a mezzanine, we behold the spinning top of a carousel,
striped red and gold. This time of year is the hardest to be barren.
Booths and shills crowd the walkways. One urges us to sample his cherry cordials.
Sticky centers crimson our mouths. The Wurlitzer is not a real Wurlitzer,
but a CD on repeat, speakers hidden inside the carousel, just as the horses
are not wood but fiberglass. Its sprightly notes mix with Nat King Cole
crooning holy infant so tender and mild.

5. The Pink Dress
I dreamed of a thirteen-year-old girl. Her back was to the light, so I couldn't see her face, but somehow, I knew she looked just like me. Against her body, she held a pink dress that I wore once, long ago. "Can I wear this, Mother?" All around us the sound of children whispering and giggling in the walls. The next morning, when I told you about the dream, you pointed out that on this day, thirteen years

ago, I had my hysterectomy. So what is there to do but take a bouquet of roses, pink as my scar, and baby's breath, to the place where we began, to the hill where my grandmother's afterbirth was buried, in the time before these streets had names. Five generations dishing up blood-red menudo and tacos de tripitas, nothing wasted. I'm afraid to not have a child is to be forever a child. I'm afraid to not have a child is a balance that can never be repaid. I'm afraid that when she reaches for me, I won't be there.

Magic Eye

When you catch my eye, I take off my glasses. That way,
there's nothing between us. Sometimes, I like things
to be not too distinct, like an impressionist painting. Light
and color and mood more important than detail. I collect
Catholic kitsch, telling myself it's ironic. St. Lucy with her eyes
on a plate. Baron Samedi with his broken sunglasses. I hold
eggs up to the light. I buy a house. Take a pregnancy test.
If a virgin can conceive, why not someone with no uterus?
I watch the minute hand, but it moves so slowly, I never quite
catch it. I take up yoga and time-lapse photography.
I search the light trails. I search the Crayola scribblings
of my nieces and nephews, hoping they will reveal something,
like those old Magic Eye posters. I could never see anything
in those either. Astigmatism. Light splinters in my vision.
My neighbor keeps chickens in a coop under her back deck. She
lets them out sometimes to flutter around the yard. They have no
concept of roads or jokes, of what came first; no notion of what
their entrails might disclose. I host a dinner party. Shuffle the cards,
pretend that I don't know that hearts correspond to cups, try not to
think about emptiness. Attend a meditation retreat where
emptiness
is the point. Start eating arugula, almost zero calories, praying for
the void to enter me. Find a god's eye in the woods, purple yarn
dangling from the naked tree branches. A way into the labyrinth.
I need eye drops in ragweed season. Grumble about the clothes
the kids are wearing these days. Build a birdhouse. Buy seed.
Cry so easily. I stand at the mouth of a forest path, where the trees
form a tunnel, trying to see if it leads somewhere other than to
asphalt and traffic lights flashing red, trying to find the pattern
in chicken scratch. In the summer, I will stand at the other end,
chasing mirages on ozone red-alert days. I think I have loved
more than I have been loved, but there's no reliable metric.
I hold Easter eggs up to the light. They lull me with their pastel
facades and promises of sweets. You have to carve your own path
to the center of God's eye. Mark the way with purple yarn, hoping
someone will follow. A demon-red fox prowls in the undergrowth,
eyes yellow-green. Stop go yield. I plan baby showers for all

my friends. I plan kids' birthday parties. Deviled eggs are my signature dish. I tattoo myself with rabbits, with hearts and bones. This is my only home so might as well feather the nest, even if I dwell here alone. Look forward to Bloody Marys and mimosas. Paint roses red. Build a pit for us to gather around the holy fire. My journey has only just begun. My glasses discarded on the bedside table. I don my sleep mask, craving perfect darkness. Infinity can only be seen with the inner eye.

Still

It was March, and the wind blew and blew.
Sound and mood, blowing the scent of you to me.
Every few minutes, I check to see
if I can still smell. So far, I can.
The pictures come over the newsfeed:
shuttered storefronts, abandoned plazas,
cancelled weddings. But the medical wards
overflow. We never imagined such confinement,
frozen, in situ, like denizens of Pompeii,
curled towards each other. They say our love
is contaminated. Still, we have the wind. Still,
we have this sycamore, these potted tulips.
Our apartment faces westward.
In the afternoons, we go out onto the balcony.
We enjoy our neighbor's wind chimes.
We wave to the other neighbor across the way,
who looks up from his book long enough
to wave back. Al fresco, clouds play shadow games
across our faces, seed pods burst
from vines along the fence at the edge
of the property. Bees probe a knothole
on the ledge at your elbow, staking out new territory.
I wonder if they can tell a board is no longer a tree.
When I grow too hot, I scoot back into the overhang,
shading my eyes from tomorrow.
Packages come like messages in a bottle,
milk and medicine on the stoop.
The workers say, this is my body,
but the store is all out of loaves.
Now I hear a run has started on seed packets.
We look out to see the delivery driver snap on
a fresh pair of gloves, purple as the irises
that have yet to bloom. We watch him drive away,
your hand in mine, dry from repeated washings.
I look down at the earth and wonder
if it's all enough, this solitude, this untapped soil,
this extended night of the tomb.

If we get desperate enough, we can eat bulbs
like they did in Arnhem. We can still smell
its clean green heart. When we look back
on this time, we will say, we were still able
to take the air. We ate supper early.
We went to bed early. This is the stone
we rolled across the entrance to our resting place.
We waited for the ash to cover us.
There was nowhere for the mourners to gather.
We'll see how it is in May. By then,
the wind will have stopped blowing, surely,
by then—

Daybreak

Sometimes,
the shaman's path
is air.
I aspire to feathers
and hollow bones,
an appetite for grubs.
Watch for my wings
at daybreak,
when I depart this earth
and sing.

Minor Arcana

The stories say you must be
born into this. If you are, wizards and
fairy godmothers eventually appear,
white rabbits, swords in stones, even
a twister to spirit you away to
your destiny. They don't tell you
some of us are born on the outskirts,
in the wrong age, cursed with awareness,
doomed to yearn for bygone magics. You
know there's something out there, but
it's hard chasing shadows in these
well-lit times, where the gardens are orderly,
where the trees are too thin for wolves,
where the hearths are strictly decorative, and
no one uses a cauldron anymore. My
madrina never conjured a pumpkin
coach, she just gave me a rosary,
and took me shoe-shopping on my
birthday. I don't look for black cats
to cross my path; I watch for the
portentous passage of deer, a certain
pattern of leaves. I squint at fireflies,
hoping to catch a pixie trying to blend.
I can trace these desires back to taking
wishes upon stars way too seriously, and
dandelion seed bursts, and he-loves-me-he-
loves-me-nots. I hurled coins into fountains,
rubbed the boar statue's snout, hunted
for talismans in thrift store discount bins. I
read all the books, lit candles, cast stones,
told myself I could almost hear the night
whispers, the ecstasy of celestial bodies
caught in their eternal dervish. I swear
I've caught idols and icons following me
with their eyes, but the fox that appears
in my yard leads me only to the vacant lot
at the end of the street, where a bulldozer

idled. All my dreams are riddles and
fortune cookies: a beggar offering me
nine gold paperclips or an old woman
in a rocking chair, warning me that I do myself
a disservice. The cards and crystal balls
do not speak to me. The planchette remains
stubbornly still. Yet, I never grow tired
of totems and moongazing, of opening doors
and boxes. I tell myself, *Revelations*
come to those who wait. I grow old.
I fill my life with teacups and spinning
wheels. After all, someone has to count the coins
and cut branches for wands. Someone must
tend the shrine, cover the mirrors. Maybe I
will never be the heroine of my own story, but
I can still be the crone in someone else's.

Ambergris

My friend gifts me a bottle of ambergris perfume.
Its musk surprises me with its chameleonic olfactory range,
reminding me sometimes of damp earth
and sometimes of root beer, sometimes of warm cookies
and sometimes of old woman, but in a good way,
of the grandmotherly scents of gardening and baking,
of dried flowers and kitchen spices. After a day,
I decide that this suits me, this grandma whale magic.
Female orcas live longer to care for their grandchildren.
Sperm whales, like elephants, live in matriarchal communities
with their calves. Mama Cocha, goddess of the sea.
Product of bile ducts, allowing beaks of squids and other
indigestibles to pass through. Forges of hardship.
Forges of survival. We take this excretion, roll it around
in the brine and the air and time. Gift of ages. Served with eggs,
it was said to be King Charles II's favorite dish. The Egyptians
burned it as incense. (I will go forth and pass through.)
The ancient Chinese called it dragon spittle.
Believed to be powerful medicine, believed to ward off plague,
some thought it was tree resin that had flowed down
through the root system, to the sea. Some believed
it came from the mountains, peaks exuding honey,
(One must go down in order to go up) making it a symbol of air
instead of water, a hand to the sky, link between heaven and earth.
Some say it's the top of the Sefirot, crown chakra, the highest self,
intermediary between God and the other emanations.
Emanations calling to emanations, as whales click and echolocate.
Jonah and the whale, purified by his stint inside the great fish,
praying, penitential, vomited out to do God's bidding.
In order to emerge, one must be swallowed whole.
I go down to the sea and await the touch of bottom teeth.
Whales have poor senses of smell, so they probably won't
be able to smell themselves on me. So I sing. I sing,
hoping that the waves will carry my voice to them,
hoping that they will take me to new depths,
teach me to swallow chiton, how to rattle hardship

in my gullet and call it nourishment, how to grind
what I can't use into something soft and precious.

Acheiropoieta
a cadralor

1. Catechism
I discovered masturbation when I was three. My mother caught me and slapped my hand,
told me I mustn't ever do that again. When I was five, I spied on an older cousin
in the shower. When I was seven, my catechism teacher told me that touching myself
was dirty and displeasing to the Lord. *Well, Lord,* I remember thinking, *this is where you and I*
part ways. The nuns, also, were quick to rap the knuckles of a budding sinner.
But I wanted to feel everything. Sometimes, I'm afraid of just how much.
There were times when I abstained, when the guilt and the shame wore me down. Now,
I can make myself come without touching. Look, Ma, no hands. It's like a loophole.
It's like tantra, fantasizing so vividly that I achieve cerebral climax, pleasure
radiating outwards from the mind, third eye unlocked. My cup runneth over.

2. Cancun
We wear the jungle air like wet silk, drink spiced honey tequila and mezcal,
agua fresca and chaya juice. Even a plunge into Ik Kil's subterranean depths does nothing
to cool our ardor. In the open-air lobby, birds rustle in the rafters, clay-colored thrushes
and doves pecking at crystals from a spilled sugar packet. A slaughter of iguanas basks
in the rock garden. In the breezeways and cafes, the waiters bring us bowls of ceviche.
We pick out bits of shrimp to share with feral cats, gorged fat as tourists on resort food.

We hop a bus to Chichen Itza. In the Mayan village, they feed us the tenderest pibil pork,
roasted in pit ovens in the Yucatan soil. The 16th century cathedral is built from pillaged stones
of former indigenous strongholds. Kulkulkan itself obscured by vendors hawking souvenirs.
My mind rings with an afterimage of a black skull wall, the clap, the nine-times echoes.

3. The Condemned
He's lived more than half his life on death row.
Now, he makes delicate origami cranes,
threads them with filaments plucked from his own meditation cushion.
He sends them to me by the envelope full. They spill forth,
scatter like stars, upcycled scrap paper, brightly-colored pages
torn from books on Buddhism. I take them out into the world and photograph them.
I leave one on a Dia de los Muertos altar, among the hundreds of other notes
left for the dead. Others I save to hang on a little white Easter tree.
They dangle like hanged men, southern trees still bearing strange fruit.
One hundred down. Only nine hundred more to go.

4. Epitaph
I don't know where any of my people are buried. I am a poor santera.
Instead, I go with you to your family plots. Sometimes, we pack a picnic,
eating pears and cheese, chocolate and almonds, in the shade of a sycamore.
We pour one out for the ancestors. Sometimes, we sweep graves, pull weeds.
The mowers have been through, they're careless about running over plastic floral
arrangements, toppling mementos. We pick up the debris, right what was desecrated.

The dead are like God. Maybe they're here; maybe they're not. Maybe they can hear us;
maybe they can't. Maybe they turn a deaf ear. We do shrooms to try and see them.
They appear, but never like you expect. I don't think they tell us anything
we don't already know: *What you are, I have been. What I am now, you will be.*

5. Soil

My grandfather was an artist. I used to play in his studio, where two mirrors
faced each other. I liked to see myself, caught in this silver crosshatch of infinity.
It's the same feeling that I get standing under a pure blue sky, looking up
into the branches of a birch, searching for nests. I eat and drink the earth.
I ask the same questions everyone has: "Can you hear me? Do you love me?"
All I hear is my own voice, echoing back, *Hear me. Love me.*
The hand and the speaker do not reveal themselves. My grandfather's hands,
like the farmer's and the pit cook's, were soiled and chapped from his labors.
You learn to read the brushstrokes and furrows.
I take up clay and begin.

MONSTERS

Supernatural

Latinos… are big moviegoers — 22 percent of audiences on any given weekend. But when it comes to horror, that proportion jumps to as much as half the box office.

-Vanessa Racaño, "Why Latinos Heart Horror Films"
NPR, October 31, 2015

They tell me Avenida Cesar Chavez used to be 23rd Street.
I don't remember that. To me, it was always just the bottom of the hill.
I remember the staircase that led from it up to Holly Street,
winding dozens of feet along the limestone bluff, skirting Gage Park,
built because it used to be a stop along the old trolley line.
My abuelo used to ride that trolley home from work.
He saw the devil there one night after a late shift.
The devil followed him almost to the top.
He was, Abuelo reported, smoking a cigarette.

The devil made many such appearances in the neighborhood.
On Summit Street, Cousin Elvira saw him in the outhouse
during a game of hide-and-seek. She was only twelve
and the experience, it was said, drove her mad.
She died in the State Hospital, raving about El Diablo.

My great-great grandmother and her sister were known santeras,
and communed with the Dark One.
They sacrificed chickens and bathed in the dirt of the yard.
They read the future from chicken entrails,
and hand-painted Tarot cards brought from the old country.
They gave you the evil eye, interpreted dreams,
and dispensed quinine-based abortifacients.

Then there was the couple who lived on Belleview.
They had a poltergeist who would pull the husband out of bed
each night, drag him outside, and deposit him,
sleepy and bewildered, in the garden. `1

On 21st Street, a widow was stalked by a specter.

When she installed a porch light, she saw it was
her deceased husband, rattling the doorknob,
tapping on windows, come to escort her to the other side.

Of course, we all knew about La Llorona,
and spent nights cowering under blankets,
afraid she would come and take us to Hell.
Her cousin, the Horse-Headed Lady, prowled the river bottoms.
It was unclear whether she also wanted children,
or just revenge for those old stockyards,
where so many hooved creatures went to their deaths.

Was it any wonder they built haunted houses
under the 12th Street Viaduct?
They opened every year mid-September,
and the owners could always count on us
to be first in line for tickets.

Of course we gathered in kitchens, on front porches.
Of course we gathered in church yards,
the children all in Catholic school uniforms,
to exchange this litany,
to whisper of otherworldly forces,
to murmur, *Ayyy* and cross ourselves.
We carried our rosaries and pinned milagros to saints' robes.
On Easter Vigil, we eagerly accepted vials of holy water,
which we sprinkled around our homes.
Not a living room without a painting of Nuestra Señora.
Not a dining room without saint candles burning on sideboards.
At summer day camp, we made Ojos de Dios,
and leather-punch wallets to carry our prayer cards in.
We went to drive-ins, hypnotized by living dolls and undead
psychopaths,
by unnamed creatures in the dark.

It wasn't all death and Satan.
Sometimes, there was divine intervention.
I can't tell if there's less of it, or if it's just harder to see.
Saints and devils change names and addresses, just like we do.

They hitchhike, hop rivers, ride shotgun on my soul.
 I will bring them forth because I must,
bearing them as I bear the weight of my bruja blood.
They came before me, and they will come after, like a scapular.
It is my turn to deliver them as they have delivered me so many times.
With new stories, I confer resurrection.

Ay de Mi

In the version my abuela told me,
she had taken a lover,
or maybe she was a widow,
on the prowl for a new husband.
In either case,
she had to get rid of her children
to please a man.
This we understood.
We knew about our mothers and their boyfriends.
Even the ones who became step-fathers
could never really see us as theirs.

Be good, or La Llorona will get you.

We could imagine it all so easily,
our little barrio by the river.
In every version,
there is always a body of water,
there is always a drowning.
This we understood as well.
Our grandfathers had crossed a river;
that's why they called us *wetbacks.*
We understood the borders
between life and not-life,
how they must be drawn
in water and breath.

Now, her restless spirit
searches endlessly
for children, calling,

¿Dónde están mis hijos?

When modern Medeas made the news,
we knew them for what they were.
Then one night, I heard it, too,
the crying.

Terrified, I hid under the covers.
My mother told me, *It's just a story,
and the sound you heard—
it was just mourning doves.*
But mourning doves don't sing at night.

If you hear La Llorona, run the other way.

Later, I realized I must have heard
a real woman crying;
those old houses built
within arm's length of each other,
open windows in the summer meant
we could hear everything
going on next door
and I didn't know a single woman
on the block
who didn't have
a reason to weep.

In some versions,
it was an act of mercy.
She'd rather see her children dead
than destitute,
bereft of love.

Now that I am a woman
who has shed her share of tears,
I understand the wandering fog,
and making choices each
more damned
than the last.

Nagual

When I was a child, you came
to devour me nightly. My mother said

I kept insisting you lived in the shadows
of the house. The claw marks on baseboards

she blamed on the dog. I told my abuela (herself
a charmer of cats) when I saw you,

prowling down 21st Street, tail twitching,
the many glimpses I caught of black flank,

always disappearing around corners,
nosing at thresholds, waiting,

with feline assurance. Such imagination,
everyone said. Where has she even seen a jaguar?

I grew older, and you went away.
I thought they must have been right:

Outsized imagination and too much appetite
for stories. I spent years – decades –

seeking darkness, without knowing
I was seeking darkness. Other animals

strayed in, and I embraced them all,
becoming jade turtle and silver-moon rabbit,

lapis-blooded, a ruby-throated hummingbird
flitting backwards and forwards in time,

borne along on my frantic wings.
I became the howlers, wolf and cicada,

shrieking in trees, sleek ermine,
puff-throated anole. So many.

I followed them through the dust,
not knowing where they led.

I didn't know all my paths
would lead back to you, westbound I-10

out of Tallahassee, and there you were,
on the frontage road. You weren't alone,

but I knew it was you. They tell me
there are no black panthers in Florida,

but I knew: lolling like a big tabby
to relieve yourself of the Southern heat.

I was nearly forty before I set foot
in Quintana Roo, in the Yucatan.

It felt like coming home. There, I fed
gentle coatis and marveled

at the slaughters of iguanas
sunning themselves in the rock garden.

At Chichen Itza, a fortune teller told me
that sun and snake and you align in me,

that I could know that which is unknown
and unknowable, the shadow self,

black as the obsidian heart of the universe.
Golden eyes blink. Twin suns,

twin eclipses. Yaguareté, you are
the truth that surpasses truth,

keystone, absolute, indisputable jaws.
Sometimes, you have to let yourself

be dragged down and devoured.
I surrender. We merge, muscle,

tooth and fur. We roll
in the red dust of sunset. I awaken

to midnight, the breath rank
in my mouth, claws snagging the bedding.

The door stands open before me
and I slink through.

Waiting for Anubis

Old enough to know better,
old enough to know
I shouldn't be courting this disaster.
Old enough to know exactly
how stupid I am.
I think of every naïf,
every ingénue,
every Fool in the spread.
I have no such excuse.
This isn't my first
conversation with a serpent.
I pack the picnic basket
with forbidden fruit
and spread my blanket
in the shade of the tombs
to wait.
The night is a black dog.
I can hear him down by the river,
his yelp through the reeds.
He will come with his butcher's scales.
Surely my heart
will be found wanting.

Medusa Browses the Beauty Aisle

She enters the sliding doors, careful to avoid
her own gaze. They call it safety glass, but she has
no illusions of safety. She takes a plastic basket
and carries it on her arm as she browses. Her fellow
shoppers instinctively give her a wide berth,
wanting to skirt both their own devastation as well as
the site of one, even though she keeps her eyes
down. All those reflective surfaces. All those
security mirrors. Fluorescent lighting pitiless
and unblinking as the eyes of old gods. The crime
is always being too beautiful, or not beautiful
enough. Her shoulders drift with dandruff,
scaly lengths of serpentine slough. She considers
coal tar. She considers Selsun Blue. She considers
chamomile, rosemary, tea tree, jojoba. But nothing
with sea salt. Never sea salt. She considers
boar-bristle brushes, hair masks, headscarves,
coconut oil. She considers banana clips and headbands.
She walks right past the straightening irons but
selects a blow dryer with a diffuser attachment.
Her snakes wriggle happily, anticipating the warm
basks to come. She samples lotions, loads up
on bath bombs, on exfoliants, on nail polish and remover,
a mani-pedi set. She tries lipsticks in shades other
than the Blood of Mine Enemies, other than
Temple Virgin Pink or Asking for It Victim,
purple as a bruise. Or maybe she just sticks
to balms, wanting comfort, wanting softness
and self-care for its own sake, exempt
from gazes now, even her own. She goes
through self-checkout, laughing to herself
at the joke.

Achilles' Fetish

After the incursion, they called me the Trojan Whore. Anyone could get inside.

As the city burned, the Acheans took hostages of a kind. Besides me, there were eight others in the brothel. The pimp was gone, either fled or slain. What was I to do? They were our enemies. They would do what they liked, whether I refused or not. If I survived the ordeal, none would take me with them. I was not even worth keeping as a slave. The only way I would sail Poseidon's rafters would be in a barrel of chum. But more likely, they would leave me behind on this ash-strewn beach, to die a traitor's death at the hands of whatever hoi polloi remained. Their desire for vengeance would demand an outlet, and is there anyone quicker to be sacrificed than a whore?

It was easier for me than for the soft ladies of Ilium. Why he picked me, I'll never know. The other men snatched at youth and beauty, and I was past my prime. But he took his time, and looked us over carefully. Something in my face must have moved him because he took my hand and led me with surprising gentleness to his tent. There, I removed his breastplate with practiced fingers, and bathed him, relieving him of the soil and sweat that accompanies a long journey. It was almost by accident that I discovered his vulnerable spot. Once found, it could not be unfound. His moans seemed to startle even him, as if he had not been aware that such pleasure existed, and in his ecstasy, he cried out, "Mother, O Mother!"

For all the days and nights he abstained from battle, I became a fixture in his tent and in his bed. How well I learned his feet, kneeling to attend the fine bones, the callused soles, the long, agile toes. I trimmed his nails for him, ran a pumice stone over the dry and hardened flesh. Gently, I massaged the hairy, muscular calves, crisscrossed with pale lines from the lacings of his sandals. I traced those lines over and over, kissed his instep. Thus I teased him, never touching his heel until last, as he writhed and shook beneath my hands. When I did, it was always with such softness, with reverence for what was mortal in my enemy. Every time, it was his undoing. I had seen (and entertained) stranger cravings in my time. I just found it extraordinary that none of his other lovers had discovered this before me. I had planted a need in him. I wondered what I would reap for it. Not even his beloved Patroclus could sate him as I could. His beloved's last action had been to encase his mortal flesh in Achilles' steel and leather, to die touching what Achilles had touched. As for Achilles, no man's blood had ever run so hot. In his grief for lost Patroclus, his rage was terrible to behold. I thought he'd destroy every living thing in his path, including me. But this is to say I feared him as much as any other man who'd ever shown me his temper. Dead is dead.

Once he spent himself, he crawled back to where I huddled. He buried his head in my lap and whispered his secrets to me, his breath hot against my thighs. How his mother, the sea nymph, she of the silver steps, had held him in the black water, the river of the dead. She dunked him like a washer woman bent over her scrubbing board. Through gritted teeth, she told him not to struggle, even as the water rushed over him, into his mouth and nostrils. He drank it down, he breathed it in. The pain of his transformation from boy to something Other was excruciating. But no matter how he cried and thrashed, she held him there. She would see her boy grow strong, to claim his godly birthright. These are the acts that birth our desires. What was done to us. What we keep reliving. As if that weren't terrible enough, there was yet another prophecy she imparted—that he would die in glorious battle, as if he would choose anything else. We are all Fate's jesters. Look at this motley flesh. How men's fates are looped together, their weft to strangle us all.

I said nothing, but stroked his hair and held him, and thought of how his mother of the glistening feet reminded me of the street girls, whose sandal-bottoms spelt out a coy *follow me* in the dirt. All men do is follow.

Spurred to fight, his need for my caresses only intensified. Whenever he returned to me after hours or days of battle, he would be wild-eyed, spattered in blood and gore. He paced impatiently through the funeral games, first for Patroclus, then for Hector, Troy's first son, whose flesh he'd threatened to eat raw. But rather than consume, he'd dragged his foe in triumphal debriding behind his chariot, and devoured me instead that night. The river choked with dead outside, such that even the river god wept. I heard it.

That night, as my captor slept, I swept up the nail clippings, the bits of skin. I gathered his hair from the bedding. I cast them into the brazier, praying to every god I could name that someone could know what I know of this man. What, to the gods, are the prayers of a whore? Maybe nothing. But what are the prayers of a whore who holds, by his tender heel, the great Achilles?

It seems I was heard. They say Apollo himself guided the arrow that slew him. But I claim that arrow. It was my prayer and my guidance. How everyone would laugh to know it was a whore who felled mighty Achilles, a whore he also called, "Mother." But rather than wait for the men, whether they be Trojans or Acheans, to finish me off, I threw myself into the wine-dark sea, and let Thetis have her way with me.

Beauty Released

I find myself at the zoo, desperate for the scent
of your musk, for salt and hay. I am drawn
to a leonine form, a flash of tusk, muscles and fur.
This is a place of captivity, of bars and glass,
of gazes, of panting. The same hands
that tend the inmates can be either gentle
or bearer of the rifle. Both are familiar to me.
Wolves pace, even the ones that were born here,
longing for something they can't put a name to.
Peacocks wander, lapis and gold, free to fly away,
but having no reason to, they stay put. Non-native plants
struggle to approximate home. We are a nation
of displacement, at the mercy of a love
we didn't choose, doomed to only be half-tamed.
Behind the petting zoo fence, I run my fingers
across coarse and woolly hides, stroke snouts,
let thick tongues lick feed from my palms.
Warm bodies lean hard against my legs.
I let myself be pounced and pecked,
clawed and butted. These bruises and bitemarks
are the memory of your arms, the push-pull
of desire that shouldn't be. Your castle kept out
as much as it kept in. The Greek gods did it.
Couldn't we be divine? I, too, can scoop water
from a trough. I, too, can eat meat raw
and howl at the moon. I go home covered
in hair and feathers, smelling of wildness.
In my bed tonight, I will dream of a pack
of chimera children.

Chthonic

The wheel of the year turns
tilting the chthonic towards us.
The underworld kingdom beckons.
I peek through its gates.
Their hymns tell
of the nowhere places.
My head becomes the eye
of a needle and the universe
threads itself through.
I am a blade of grass
about to meet the mower.
I am dust under the feet of gods.
I am new-born. I am dying.
I am giving birth to myself.
Everything is forever and never
and always.
I mourn for everything I have lost.
I mourn for what never was.
The hymns tell of ribbons and strings,
the uncuttable threads.
On the mantle, the ashes turn back
into my loved ones.
On my altar, the Anubis idol topples.

The Fable of the Tiger
after a Hmong tapestry

A man slew a monkey
with a tiger as the only witness.
The tiger killed the man –
whether in retaliation or
merely seizing an opportunity,
it is not clear –
but he took the man's clothes,
and thus disguised,
joined the world of men.
This tells us what we already know:
that men are just beasts in textiles.

Of a Feather
for Gabi Mann

Myth, fable, folklore, legend—
this is how they're born,
with an unusual child,
a connection to the animal world.
It can still happen, even in our time.

The crow was the only creature
who survived the Great Flood,
the coming of the third age of man.

It started with an accident,
a messy preschooler, a bit of dropped food.
Then she began to share with them,
morsels from her lunchbox
on the way to the bus stop.

In a pinch, may our wits serve us,
the way a few dropped pebbles in a pitcher
becomes an epiphany, and the thirsty crow
drinks.

Then her back yard became a shrine,
offerings of water and peanuts,
like the Temple of the Rats in Rajasthan,
feeding creatures that some call pests
and some call mischief, some call God
and some call darkness.

This is the story of how the crow's rainbow feathers
turned black, and his once-beautiful voice
went hoarse forever.

Grateful, the crows bring baubles,
which she catalogs, as if it were a royal treasury:
here is the heart-shaped button of pearl,
here is half a friendship charm,

here are screws and bits of metal,
here are Legos and marbles,
here are the river-polished courtship stones.

It is said that the spirit of King Arthur lives on
in the form of a crow.

The birds watch her, watching them.
They return a lost camera lens,
but only after washing it first
in the bird bath. I wonder if she feels
protected, even as she protects them,
a princess with her loyal guard.

Once upon a time, there was a girl
who loved crows, and they loved her.

Which begs the question,
are they her power animal or
is she theirs? Do the crows tell,
amongst themselves, the tale
of a hungry murder and
a beneficent human child,
or perhaps the coming of a great crow,
born in the guise of a maiden?

The girl didn't know it,
but the crows' gifts would eventually
weave a spell that would turn her back
into her true form.

Now the neighbors complain about the mess,
about clogged gutters and drainpipes,
the accumulation of feathers and droppings
and peanut shells. The magical and
the mundane have always had
so little tolerance for each other.
I hope she is learning their language.
I hope she is already weaving the tale

she will leave behind.
One day, she would have to choose.

Walkers between worlds eventually
must settle, and what girl doesn't dream
of flight, of prophecy,
of spreading her wings
and departing this world for home?

In time, the crow pierces us all.

Pisces
for Eve Brackenbury

Frozen rivers slow twin tails,
Ice stoppering gills
Shooting inlets

Silver and splendid
We leap the floes
Delivering goddesses to shore:

Sharers and renewers,
We are fishers of men.
Love is what comes

Of this dead season;
Shedding our scales
We tread the land,

Melting ice beneath our feet
So it runs back into the earth
We are the life-bringers.

We make our table on snow banks.
We are what awaits around March's bend
When standing pools reflect again

Only blue skies.

Girl with a Cigarette
after Louisiana Zombie Afternoon, *by Jenn Zed*

All the world is drowned in red.
The gun smokes. I smoke.
I hold the smoking gun in hand.
I am a smoking gun.
My Sunday dress,
the Southern sun.

Do you smell the dead,
or is it just the bayou,
its wetness and decay?
The smoke keeps
the biting flies at bay.

Annihilating sun,
even the bald cypress become
splinters in your light,
and the wild pig bones
picked clean,
tusks discarded in the muck.

I envy the dead,
impervious to all but hunger.
They hunt. I hunt.
To end them all,
or become one of them--
I haven't decided yet.

Girl Alone
after Louisiana Zombie Afternoon, *by Jenn Zed*

One-stoplight towns blink yellow and red.
The world has gone topsy-turvy
when it's the dead who are on the move
and the living have gone to ground.
Somewhere in between, I walk
these rural routes, this event horizon,
a great big nothin'. All sludge and blood
beneath a crimson sky.
I'm on my way to what lies beyond.
I'm on my way to look at God.
Old fenceposts crack a crooked smile.
Empty mailboxes gape.
Skeletal airboats succumb slowly
to boggy bottoms.
Somewhere, the last biscuit
has been lifted from the skillet.
Somewhere, the last laundry
has been taken from the line.
The fellowship halls now ring with silence.
I never thought it would be possible
to miss so much.
I never imagined how quickly
I would be over it.
This is my world now:
these ball-bearing afternoons,
this cigarette.
The stink of the gun
and the burning in my lungs
assure me that I ain't dead yet.
On the edge of the bay,
the buoy lights still bob and flash.
I walk into the water,
singing new hymns.

Girl with a Gun

after Louisiana Zombie Afternoon, *by Jenn Zed*

Of course it would happen here. Nobody was surprised
when the dead came for Louisiana. We are known
for our strange history, for saints and voodoo,
for vampires and delta blues (the best music
to die by), for jazz funerals (the best music
to waltz into heaven by), and for burying our departed
in cement bone boxes to escape the water
that's constantly threatening to suck us under,
the green Gulf that sits higher than our greatest city.
We are known for the hurricanes, for the thousands
lost in the flood. We are known for the bayous and
the wet savannas, where the pelicans and egrets
make their roosts, where the tree frogs sing
to the night and the delicate orchids thrive
on dark alluvium and rot. Where the black mold
overtakes the walls and the noxious kudzu
continues to encroach with its violet blooms.
Where the gators and the hogs and the black bears
and the painters and the canebreaks and the pinesnakes
and the fire ants and the brown recluse all wait
for their opportunity to gore and gut you. Where the ripe
and the rancid live cheek-and-jowl. Where the living
take and take, and we have always known that the dead
would come to cash in someday. But here, we have also
the coyote and the turkey vulture. We have the humble
carrion beetle. We have a girl with a gun, who is
an orchid in knee socks, who is a life-bomb
waiting to go off. We are on your trail.
Your stench is unmistakable.

GENERAL WEIRDNESS

Luna

An enviable transcendence

seven days of sheer passion

born with no purpose

but hunger
and the means to fulfill it

no mouths   only

the embrace

of aloe-soft wings

Parisian Phoenix, by Way of Texas

You write to me from death row that you
are hungry for material.
Anything will do, you say,
junk mail, newspaper clippings,
scratch paper, anything
that can be incorporated into your art,
anything to feather your concrete nest.
I understand this, how all artists
are essentially magpies at heart,
gathering shiny things and squirreling them away
as we consider the perfect setting for them,
as we consider how to make the scavenged
into something wholly new.
I select greeting cards with gems and googly eyes,
with glitter and bright colors.
I send fine stationery and postcards.
I fish discarded scrapbooking paper from a bin
with kitschy French designs:
loopy script saying *l'amour, chocolat,*
the Eiffel Tower, Notre Dame.
I send it to you anyway and you
fold a sheet of it into three paper cranes
and burn them around the edges.
You send them to another pen pal in Paris,
who ventures down to the Île de la Cité,
braving the lead dust to photograph himself
holding them, as if in offering,
as if about to let them fly,
before the doors
of the fire-damaged cathedral.
I wonder if you meant for there to be
a phoenix for each of us,
widely separated by distance and
varying degrees of freedom,
by varying degrees of emergence,
united by this burning need to rise
from our ashen chrysalis and say,

"I was here the year Notre Dame burned,
I was still here, and on a plume
of toxic chemicals, I shall be undone,
only to return."

Hair Work
after Leila's Hair Museum, Independence, MO

It was the age of taxidermy and Madame Tussaud's.
Romantic love was still newfangled,
like Proctor & Gamble's marvelous soap—
it might have scented these freshly gathered tresses,
along with macassar oil or egg yolk or lye.

Bouquets of keratin we exchanged,
boiled with baking soda, and dried,
leaving us these sentimental materials
in amber van Gogh hues: haystack and wheatfield,
boot leather, crow, sunflower heart.
We wove them into brooches and watch fobs,
bracelets and wreaths, applied wax and shellac
to keep them from frizzing, but otherwise
they needed no preservatives;
objects of unknowable tensile strength,
like spider silk connecting the living with the living,
and the living with the dead.

This strange, proto-macrame craze,
a little bit Miss Havisham,
steeped in memory, genteelly moldering,
a little bit Jack the Ripper,
his particular brand of body horror.

The shaft, you see, is already dead.
The follicle is all that lives, and it's been uprooted
for the sake of these tokens,
love and mourning always entwined,
for whenever my love is absent,
I am in mourning. But the hair endures.
So long as we have these pieces of each other,
so, too, do we endure.

Learning to Floss

At almost forty,
I'm finally learning to adult.
They say it's never too late
to unfuck yourself,
but they're wrong.
Some damage is irreparable.
When I started to floss,
it took weeks before I stopped
spitting blood in the sink.
They say my generation
is dying faster
than the generation
that came before.
That I believe.
For them, forty
was the new thirty.
I missed that cut-off.
Looking down the barrel of years
that may already be half-over,
I think how I will never
run a marathon,
never have savings
or a retirement fund,
never have a house or a child,
never learn to change a tire
or the oil in my car,
never learn to eat the salad
or drink the wine.
But flossing, now--
flossing I've got down,
along with
how to get evicted,
how to lose everything,
how to suffer
and witness suffering,
how to catalog my scars,
how to crawl

out of the wreckage.
They tell you that you
have the power,
but you don't.
That's why we're all
riddled with anxiety.
Helplessness is trauma.
They never tell you
that if you want
to walk among the stars
you have to withstand
the vacuum of space.
That's what this suffering
supposedly prepares you for,
passage through needles' eyes
and treading holy eight-fold paths.
I don't know if it's a talent
particular to me,
or if it's all just context,
like a generation selling out,
beating their peace signs
into stock symbols,
like riding camels to some
imaginary kingdom,
like spitting
from the backs of stars.

The Holy Sweet

For over 300 years,
in a secret temple kitchen
in Andhra Pradesh,
they have made
this humble confection:
chickpea flour, clarified butter,
sugar, cashew nuts,
raisins and cardamom.
The sacred tirupati laddu,
offering to Venkateswara.
To make it is both an honor
and a responsibility
awarded only to a few
select cooks. The recipe
is top secret. When freshly made,
it should weigh exactly
178 grams. As it cools, it reduces
to 174. Such precision,
such reverence. To partake,
one must undertake a pilgrimage.
Only a few rupees, about 15 cents apiece,
limit three per customer.
Over 300,000 a day served,
a gamut of high-tech coupons
with facial recognition,
of long lines made up
of the faithful or merely
the famished. It is one of the few
products of the world that merits
a GI tag, like champagne
or Darjeeling tea.
Accept no substitutes.
Make your offering
first to the deity,
then you may consume it.
If you want to taste
what God tastes,

if you want to have
your sins destroyed,
you must prove
yourself worthy.

Priestess

Nasca Hair, Peru – the skull of a woman, possibly a priestess, with hair still attached, from approximately 200 BCE. The hair is 2.8 meters long. (Museum of Archaeology, Anthropology, and History of the UNT, Trujillo, Peru)

Over 9 feet of hair, it lies
in two long ropes,
turning and twisting in on itself
like the branches of a huarango tree.
Even now, the average height for women in Peru
is only 5'2". Imagine having hair
almost twice as long as your body.
Priestess, what must your life have been
for you to sweep about
with such epic locks?
The heft of it! The heat of it!
And what a job it must have been
to wash. I wonder if you
had attendants to follow you around,
keeping your follicular train
from dragging along the floor,
or if you carried it yourself,
draped over your shoulders
like a stole? Or did you spend
all your time in the temple,
lost in the ecstasy
of mescaline cactus visions,
dancing with your killer whale
and spotted cat gods,
with your gods of fish
and peanuts, with the three sisters
crop avatars?

A climate of extremes
begets a culture of excess:
immense earthworks and plazas,
the famous lines scrawled
for miles across the desert

that were clearly meant
for gods' eyes. So we can't exactly
claim surprise to find such hair—
equally massive, equally deliberate.
These tresses suggest, too,
the puquios, stone spirals running
into the earth. In a time when water
and God were inextricable,
did you swim the aethereal channel,
bringing divinity back down to earth
to slake the thirst of the faithful?
O priestess of trepanation,
of cranial modification,
collector of trophy heads,
what strange phrenology
must you represent? With your language
of knotted strings, the natural argot
of weavers, your warp and weft
are equally indecipherable.

Are you the Nasca, the Andes?

Are you the Earth itself?

Eventually, despite your efforts,
drought took them all.

Now you're housed
in the same museum,
(a temple of sorts),
beside the effigy of a woman
carved out of whale's tooth.
It, too, has hair. Maybe you knew
that bone and hair persist,
that it would be the tether
between past and future,
between us and you,
the last echo of your magic.

Cursed Images
an ekphrastic poem, of a sort

Old man in a wood-paneled room with crates of tomatoes.
Display tables made of two-by-fours and oil drums.

Not cursed like Cain or King Tut's tomb;
not cursed like a thespian dooming himself
by uttering the name of the Scottish play.
Nor is it that you, viewer, are the one who's cursed
for looking upon them,
like Ham beholding his father's shame.

A crude cross covered in black garbage bags.
Crucified to it a naked Barbie.

It's that there are places – moments –
in this world that are cursed.
Sometimes, they are only a few feet wide,
an anomaly of physics,
like Santa Cruz's Mystery Spot,
where gravity and perspective seem to bend
in the uncanny hush of redwoods.
They're there for just an instant,
then gone again.

A woman at a kitchen counter slicing salami
with an old Windows XP disc.

The internet, like all communities,
has spawned its own lore,
spoken in the language it knows best:
let us bring you disquiet in pixels.

A herd of sheep at dusk, beneath an orange and charcoal sky.
Dozens of pairs of glowing eyes bore into you.

The unease that you crave.
All nightmares are composed of fragments

of real life. Your mind gives them
back to you, off-kilter. Why do we seek it out?
Oh, we like novelty. We like sensation.

A man wearing a hollowed-out koala bear plushie
as a mask, casually sipping beer through a straw,

Violent content teaches us about violence.
It's a defense mechanism.
Feeling creeped out is just the body's response
to something ambiguous, when something's
not quite right and you can't put your finger
on why. The mind hovers, unable to light.
Friend or foe? Threat, or not a threat?
Real or unreal?

A crowd of gray aliens.
There's a woman standing behind them for scale.
They're just children in costumes—aren't they?

Existential horror. Cosmic horror.
A place where other universes bleed
into this one, or a bend in the U-joint
between heaven and hell, and it's
so very hard to tell sometimes
what is real.

Night cam. A child, barefoot,
wearing a nightgown,
standing with two deer,
in the middle of a forest.
Too still. They might be angels
or ghosts or demons.

Monsieur Daguerre who first captured
the Boulevard du Temple
in copper and silver and iodine
could never have imagined this:
our reality now composed of images.

Pics or it didn't happen. We live
in images. We feed on images.
1.2 trillion digital photos will be taken this year.
More photos taken every two minutes
than there were taken in the entirety
of the 18th century.
Some pictures
would take on a life of their own.
A life means a personality.
Not all personalities are friendly.

A dank basement with a table, dolls arranged
around it in the manner of The Last Supper.
Coins scattered on the tabletop.
You would think they were 30 pieces of silver
but they're not. Just plain old Lincoln pennies,
dull with tarnish.

Some Native Americans and Aborigines
still refuse to be photographed.
The Kayapos of the Amazon call photography
akaron kaba, "to steal a soul."
The Amish believe photos are graven images.
We give our souls every day
for selfies and profile shots.
We make of ourselves graven images.

A shopping mall fountain geysers what,
at first glance, appears to be blood.
Water dyed blood-red.
Undoubtedly a St. Valentine's Day miscalculation,
a celebration of a sports team with red jerseys.
Or blood. It could be blood.

They say you photograph anything
that you can't bear to lose.
Time is the fire in which we burn
and photographs are our way
of rushing back into the flames

to salvage our keepsakes.
A scar is also a keepsake.
Our brains cling to the hurt.
Nothing teaches like a hurt.
Masochism a necessity.

A suburban lawn overrun by badgers.

The world is wrong. It's nice to know
that no, we're not crazy.
It's really, really wrong.
In a time of Photoshop and filters
and deep fakes, this unblinking ugliness
is almost a comfort.
Art used to hold a mirror up to society.
Now, we live inside that mirror.

Dysfunctional furniture. Odd food combinations.
Dolls and mannequins. Masks and costumes.
Eerie hallways. Dark and empty rooms.
A necklace of human teeth.
Crepuscular creatures. Uncanny faces
captured by front door cams.

What is wrong. What is wrong. What is wrong.
We are. We are. We are.
We are wrong. And we juxtapose.
And we are absurd. And we squirm.

A staircase in the middle of a forest
that has no business being
in the middle of a forest.
Not a foundation stone nor any other
parts of a building in sight.
Just stairs. Leading up to nowhere.
Leaves collecting in the risers.

Except we are the slayer of our brother,
the brazen archaeologist disturbing

the pharaoh's eternal rest. Except we are
Macbeth, Macbeth, Macbeth,
rubbernecking at Noah's drunken shenanigans.

An old black and white photo,
1960s Butterick dresses and Formica.
Two nice-looking ladies having lunch with a nun.
The nun's eyes a diabolical flash.

We are the technology as
the creator is us,
which means God is also
dirt and God is also
cursed
with us.

White Noise

Mid-winter
just like every winter,
when we all become fascinated
with the freezing point of water,
when we all become experts
on weather patterns,
on the nature of asphalt under
extreme conditions.
When the weather man
becomes a permanent fixture
on our TV screens.
When everybody says,
Be careful going home,
and really means it.
When I look out the window
and wonder if we are
the product of our environment,
am I this polar vortex?
Am I these prevailing winds?
Am I this pale void?
Or am I just
white noise?
And I shiver.

Metaphysics and Bananas
after The Uncertainty of the Poet *by Giorgio de Chiroco*

I feel this indecision:
am I a banana,
alone, or in a bunch?
Certainly anonymous,
certainly not autonomous.
Am I a statue,
chalk-white with ages,
headless and limbless,
just tits and ass?
Yes, I am a looker.
Yes, I am gazeless.
Stone collides
with the stoneless,
the easily mushed.
These are my choices?
Is that a choo-choo coming,
rattle and clack,
my ship coming in,
faceless, launched?
What door should I be
slouching towards?
If I go in, is there any guarantee
I'll come out again?
I don't have to be frozen.
I don't have to lie here, scattered,
creeping towards impending rot,
having never known the pleasure
of being peeled and eaten,
of being halved for the I scream
you scream and a cherry
on top. I don't
have to watch
the shadows creep
despite that blue sky.
I am form.
I can have both:

these marble bones and this
highly bruisable skin.
I can be clad only
in dimples and folds,
testament of bygones,
when the cushion still pushed,
sustenance unconsumed.
My trunk implies
I am rootless,
a turn-about fair player,
both goer and stayer,
lingerer at thresholds.
Yes, the dark is light.
Yes, it's now, then.
Yes, these stairs lead down
into dirt, or else water.
A cut branch gives at least
one last time. This shoot
may latch again.
The answer is always
depart.
Depart.
Depart.

The Gilded Monk

after a 1,000-year-old mummified monk found hidden in statue

Hundreds tried but only 24 ever achieved
what the Japanese called *sokushinbutsu,*
the act of self-mummification:
3,000 days of brutal preparation.
First, limit your diet to nuts, seeds, bark, and roots.
Perform strenuous physical activity to further
pare down the body. Drink toxic Urushi tea.
It will make you vomit, but it will also
make your remains impervious to maggots
and the bacteria that feed on corpses.
When you are ready, your pine box
is just large enough for you
to fold yourself into the lotus position.
We lower you into the ground,
a bamboo tube for oxygen.
Every day, you ring a bell to let us know
that you are still alive.
When the bell stops ringing,
we know to remove the tube
and seal you in. In 1,000 days,
we exhume you.

You are found preserved.
You achieved the death-trance.
Now a holy object, you are moved
to the temple to be revered
until it is time for you to awaken.

1,000 years later,
your body is found in Amsterdam,
tucked inside a statue of the Buddha
with scrolls of paper
where your lungs once were.
This cannot be your terminus—
garish gold leafing and papier-mâché,
museum tours across Europe.

Where does your soul yet sojourn?
Do you yet dwell among the devas,
gathering sufficient wisdom
to deliver salvation unto us?

We await you, bodhisattva.
We speak your name, Liuquan.

Under the Periwinkle

Some call it
the graveyard vine,
groundcover that, once
planted and mulched,
asks so little, unfazed
by shade, by the cold
of winter months, by
the acidity or basicity
of decomposing bodies;
in return, it rushes in
where turf and fescue
fail to thrive, smothering
weeds. It stays low,
giving the appearance
of capitulation, pallid
blooms the color
of hush, fit for repose.
Imagine anchoring
down through the old
winding sheets and
pine boxes, friending
the succulent and long-lived
Spanish Dagger, with its
down-facing white clusters,
bulbs, cedar, iris and aster;
perennials and evergreens
we plant among the departed
like wishes, like portkeys,
semaphores to signal them back,
to show them that it can
be done. Lost or forgotten
sites, lacking tombstones,
can be found again,
the past navigable by these
blue-white-lavender stars,
firmament at our feet,

kingdom come held
in petals and stems.

Where Man Doth Not Inhabit
for melting Antarctica

Austral summers devoid of stars
save one; only mountains preside
over the dust and salt, the scouring cold,
the nothing that is not nothing,
only not mammal. What rough materials
keep their secrets--
it may seem like proof of our solitude
until the wind moves down the slopes
like a goading hand. We stand
in the shadow of the observatory.
Land of the unseen,
connecting us to other worlds,
umbilicus of bacteria and protein,
soil around us littered
with the universe's fallen messengers.
O, world's beginning and world's end,
so far from the borders of man,
we've forgotten our kinship
to the pared-down and the open,
bottom rung on the ladder
to cosmic radiance.
The second season comes.
Driven indoors by the killing cold,
we sleep, like microbes in ice,
we sleep. Thaw us out and we
hatch color.

Trypophobia
a cadralor

1. For my 8th birthday, I got a Nintendo.
I could always tell when it was on. Even from downstairs,
I could feel the low, electrical pulse of it
buzzing in my teeth.

2. It's tornado season again. The wind chimes do more than dance.
They judder and jangle in a frantic melody, more warning than the
sirens:
the world goes dark and the sky is green. Everything is about to
upend.
Seek the low, interior places.

3. I am the moist pink gum bed,
raw jolt of exposed nerve endings,
tongue probing the gap,
charting absence.

4. The Wi-Fi spirits whisper, *See?*
We've been telling you all along
that distance and time don't matter.
Soon you won't even need the machine.

5. I have always hated tunnels and burrows. Hate them, but I can't
look away.
I have to know what's on the other side, yearning for gateways, an
escape hatch.
I pick up abandoned keys and pocket them. I want to melt through
the honeycomb
of interlocking universes, become one with the hole.

Acknowledgements

These poems have appeared or are forthcoming in *One Hand Clapping, Pensive, The Rye Whiskey Review, GLEAM: A Journal of the Cadralor, The Dope Fiend Daily, CultureCult Magazine, 1870 Review, Setu Magazine, Rough Cut Press, POETiCA REViEW, Anvil Tongue Books, Lothlorien Journal, The Racket, Hole in the Head Review, Life and Legends, Art in the Time of COVID-19, Heron Clan VII, Madness Muse Press, Making Waves, The Winnow Magazine: Catalogued Pains, Lethe Literary and Art Journal, Io Literary Journal, The Wild Word, The Ekphrastic Review, Unearthed, The Turnip Truck(s), Stanzaic Stylings, MacQueen's Quinterly, Gnashing Teeth, Ice Floe,* and *Unlikely Stories Mark V.*

Honors

"Beauty Released," Best of the Net nominee, 2021, Anvil Tongue Books

"Acheiropoieta," Pushcart Prize nominee, 2020; Best of the Net nominee, 2021, *GLEAM: A Journal of the Cadralor*

"Priestess," Pushcart Prize nominee, 2021; Rhysling Award nominee, 2022, *Lothlorien Journal;* 2022 Stephen A. DiBiase Poetry Contest Finalist

"Nagual," Pushcart Prize nominee, 2021, *The Winnow Magazine*

The Lumiere Review Contest Top 100, 2021 – for a selection of poems, including "Of a Feather" and "Portrait of an Amateur Roadkill Artist"

About the Author

Lauren Scharhag (she/her) is an award-winning author of fiction and poetry, and a senior editor at *Gleam*. Her titles include seven poetry collections. The latest, *Midnight Glossolalia* (with Scott Ferry and Lillian Necakov) is now available from Meat for Tea Press. She has received multiple Best of the Net, Pushcart Prize, and Rhysling Award nominations. She lives in Kansas City, MO. https://linktr.ee/laurenscharhag